Protecting Your Growth:
Cybersecurity Basics for Small Business Owners

Gustavo Leszczynski

Table of Contents

Chapter 1: The Importance of Cybersecurity for Small Businesses

There are an increasing number of online hazards to small enterprises in this internet-connected world. Cybersecurity refers to the process of safeguarding your electronic devices, networks, and data against various dangers. When compared to huge organizations, small businesses usually have lower defenses, making them easy prey for hackers. Despite this, many small business owners still believe their company is too tiny to be attacked.

Picture this: you run a mom-and-pop bakery and keep track of all your orders, customers' details, and money on a computer. You open an email that appears to be from a supplier; nevertheless, your computer becomes infected with a virus the moment you click on the link within. This malware has the potential to steal sensitive client information, encrypt your computer, and then demand a ransom in order to decrypt it. A lot of mom-and-pop stores are in danger from this.

Facts to Think About: The majority of small business owners (88%) feel their company may be targeted by a cyberattack, according to the Small Business Administration. Additionally, small firms are the targets of 43% of cyberattacks, according to a Verizon research. These figures show how critical it is to treat cybersecurity with the seriousness it deserves.

Understanding Cyber Threats

Here are a few typical cyber dangers and how they work:

Phishing: Phishing is when someone tries to trick you into giving them your personal information, like passwords or credit card numbers. They often do this by sending you fake emails that look like they are from a legitimate company.

Example: You receive an email that looks like it's from your bank, asking you to click on a link and enter your account details. If you do, the scammers can steal your money.

Ransomware: Ransomware is a type of software that blocks access to your data or systems until you pay a ransom to the attacker.

Example: A small medical practice in California was hit by ransomware, and they couldn't access their patient records until they paid the attackers $75,000 in Bitcoin.

Malware: Malware is any software designed to harm your computer or steal your information. This includes viruses, spyware, and trojans.

Example: A retail business unknowingly downloaded malware that stole customer credit card information, resulting in over $100,000 in fines and lost business.

Business Email Compromise (BEC): BEC is when someone pretends to be a trusted person or company to trick you into sending them money or sensitive information.

Example: A small law firm received an email that seemed to be from a trusted client, but it was actually from an attacker who stole sensitive client information after the firm's lawyer entered their login details.

Why Small Businesses Should Care

Financial Loss: Cyber-attacks can be very costly. According to Hiscox, a single cyber-attack can cost a small business over $200,000. This includes not just the money paid to attackers, but also the cost of repairing systems, lost revenue, and legal fees.

Reputation Damage: If your business is hacked and customer information is stolen, it can damage your reputation. Customers may lose trust in you and take their business elsewhere.

Operational Disruption: Cyber-attacks can disrupt your daily operations, making it impossible to access important data or systems. This can lead to lost sales and productivity.

Legal Consequences: Depending on your industry, you may face legal consequences if you fail to protect customer data. Regulations like the General Data Protection Regulation (GDPR) in Europe and the California Consumer Privacy Act (CCPA) have strict requirements for data protection.

Simple Steps to Improve Cybersecurity

Use Strong Passwords: Passwords that are strong are lengthy (containing 12 characters or more) and have a combination of letters, numbers, and symbols. Do not use "password" or "123456" as your password.

Try something more complex, such "B@k3ry!&%2021," as your password instead of "bakery123."

Enable Two-Factor Authentication (2FA): Through the use of a second verification method, such as a code delivered to your phone, two-factor authentication increases the security of a login.

The second factor ensures that your account remains secure even in the event that your password is compromised.

Keep Software Updated: Security patches are a common component of software upgrades. Always use the most recent versions of your operating system, programs, and antivirus protection.

Make sure you're running the most recent security patches by setting your computer to install updates automatically.

Backup Your Data: Use a cloud service or an external hard drive to back up your data on a regular basis. You can simply recover your data in the event that it is stolen or lost.

Make sure you back up your crucial files using services like Dropbox or Google Drive, or use an external hard drive.

Put Your Employees in the Know: Train your staff on a regular basis to recognize questionable emails and take appropriate action when faced with them.

Why These Strategies Work

Strong Passwords and 2FA: Protect Your Accounts from Unauthorized Access by Using Strong Passwords and Two-Factor Authentication (2FA).

Software Updates: Protect yourself from known vulnerabilities that attackers could exploit by keeping your software updated. Sixty percent of the breaches discovered in the 2020 Verizon Data Breach Investigations Report had vulnerabilities for which fixes were available but not implemented.

Data Backups: Regular backups ensure a quick recovery if data is ever lost, stolen, or corrupted by a computer failure. Surprisingly, 70% of firms have suffered downtime as a result of data loss, according to the Global Data Protection Index. A basic yet essential measure to safeguard your important data is to establish a backup practice.

Employee Education: Educating your employees can significantly reduce the risk of successful cyber-attacks. Strong training and awareness programs see a 70% decrease in security incidents caused by human error, according to the SANS Institute.

Making Cybersecurity a Priority

Everyone who owns a small business should prioritize cybersecurity. Your company might be safeguarded against possible dangers by way of easy, preventative measures. In addition to protecting your financial security, this will earn your clients' trust and keep your business running efficiently.

Case in Point: A ransomware assault encrypts all client data at a tiny marketing business. Thankfully, they were able to recover their data without having to pay the ransom since they kept frequent backups. Their aggressive cybersecurity measures were highlighted by this occurrence.

Particularly for less tech-savvy small company owners, cybersecurity might appear to be an insurmountable obstacle. You can lessen the likelihood of cyberattacks by learning the fundamentals and putting them into practice. Avoiding short-term losses is important, but safeguarding your company against cyber risks is critical to its continued success and expansion in the long run.

You will gain a better understanding of the many cyber dangers, how to safeguard your company, and how to establish a cybersecurity culture as you go through this book. The point of incorporating cybersecurity into your routine is for it to become automatic for both you and your staff.

Chapter 2: Understanding the Basics of Cybersecurity

What is Cybersecurity and Why Does It Matter?

Cybersecurity refers to the process of safeguarding information and electronic systems, networks, data, and devices from intrusion. To put it simply, it's the same as securing your home's doors and windows with locks. You shouldn't let unauthorized people into your digital systems any more than you would let them into your home.

Nowadays, it seems like everything has an internet connection. There is a flood of sensitive information kept online, ranging from financial and social security numbers to trade secrets and intellectual property. Cybersecurity is essential for protecting this data from unwanted access, theft, or damage.

Common Types of Cyber-Attacks

Phishing

Cybercriminals engage in phishing when they attempt to deceive victims into divulging sensitive information (such as login credentials, passwords, and financial data) by impersonating a legitimate business or organization. Criminals frequently use phishing emails, websites, and text messages to do this. If your bank impersonates an email and requests that you change your password, for instance, you may fall for the scam. Attackers can now access your account if you click the link and input your data.

Case in point: Envision yourself getting an email that appears to have originated from your bank, down to the logo and formatting. Your account has been the target of suspicious behavior, according to the email, therefore you must instantly confirm your details. Concerned, you follow the link, only to be sent to a website that closely resembles your bank's. When you log in, you may believe you are protecting your account, but in fact, a hacker has just gained access to your sensitive data.

In 2020, 241,343 distinct phishing websites were identified, according per the Anti-Phishing Working Group. In 2020, 241,342 people in the US fell prey to phishing, making it the most prevalent kind of cybercrime, according to the FBI.

Ransomware

Ransomware is malicious software that encrypts your files or locks you out of your computer. After that, the hacker will ask for payment, usually in bitcoin, to decrypt your files or unlock your system. Even if you pay the ransom, it won't restore access and will only encourage the thieves to keep stealing.

Case in point: Ransomware known as WannaCry in 2017 infected a large number of systems throughout the globe. The cyberattack encrypts data and demands Bitcoin ransom from systems running Microsoft Windows. A wide range of organizations were affected, including hospitals, corporations, and government institutions, leading to extensive disruption.

According to Cybersecurity Ventures, the yearly cost of ransomware will reach $265 billion USD by 2031, up from $42 billion in 2024 and $20 billion in 2021. They also predict that ransomware attackers will launch a new attack on consumers or organizations every two seconds, and that their malware payloads and related extortion activities will continue to evolve.

Malware

Any piece of software whose primary goal is to harm computers, servers, clients, or networks is known as malware. Included in this category are spyware, Trojan horses, worms, and viruses. Threat actors can gain control of your system, steal important information, or halt operations by using malware.

Trojan horses are prevalent forms of malware that masquerade as official software. An example of this would be a Trojan horse that masquerades as a free game but really gives hackers access to your system and all of your private data.

Malware is quite common. The number of malware programs deployed globally exceeds one billion, as reported by the AV Test Institute. More than 560,000 new pieces of malware are discovered every day.

Social Engineering

The goal of social engineering is to trick someone into giving up sensitive information or doing some sort of action against their will. Social engineering differs from more conventional forms of cyberattacks in that it takes use of human nature, including altruism and the need to respond rapidly.

By instilling a sense of urgency, attackers take advantage of these human instincts. For instance, they may phone an employee and pretend to be from an established company, such as IT assistance, and say there's a critical problem with their account. The perpetrator can coerce the worker into divulging their password or allowing access to confidential systems by instilling a feeling of urgency and dread.

Case in point: An imposter contacts a worker by pretending to be an IT help representative. According to them, the employee's account is experiencing a significant problem that needs fixing right now. Under pressure to "fix" the issue, the attacker obtains the employee's password and gains access to the company's network.

How Cyber-Attacks Can Affect Small Businesses

It is a common but mistaken belief among small businesses that they are immune to cybercrime. Actually, tiny firms are easy prey since they don't usually have the strong security systems that bigger corporations have. Cyber-attacks can have the following effects on small businesses:

Financial Loss

Cyber-attacks have the potential to cause substantial monetary damages. Consider the following scenario: your company's operations may come to a halt due to the inability to access your systems, caused by a ransomware assault. Paying the ransom adds insult to injury, because this outage might cause income to drop.

Case in point: Ransomware encrypts all client records at a tiny accounting business. They were held hostage until they paid a $10,000 Bitcoin ransom to get their files back. A major financial loss occurred because of the ransom and the loss of a week's worth of commercial activities.

A whopping 41% of small firms were hit by cyber attacks in 2023, according to the Hiscox Cyber Readiness Report. Cyber assaults cost small businesses an average of $8,300 a year.

Reputation Damage

Customer confidence in your company might take a major hit in the event of a data leak caused by a cyberattack. Customers have high expectations for the security of their personal information; any compromise may cause them to lose trust and loyalty.

In 2020, 87% of customers said they would go elsewhere if they didn't trust a firm to appropriately handle their data, according to a poll by PwC.

Case in point: A data breach occurred at a tiny online store, exposing the names, addresses, and credit card details of customers. When word got out about the hack, it caused a drop in consumer confidence and unfavorable press. The company had a hard time getting back on its feet after losing a lot of clients.

Legal Consequences

Businesses must ensure the security of client data in accordance with many laws and regulations. Fines and lawsuits are among the legal ramifications that may result from a data breach. As an example, data breaches can result in severe penalties under the EU's General Data Protection Regulation (GDPR).

Overall, data breaches cost an average of $3.86 million in 2020, according to IBM's Cost of a Data Breach Report. Even a small percentage of this amount can be catastrophic for small enterprises, which often encounter smaller expenditures.

Case in point: A data leak compromised the privacy of patients' medical records at a small healthcare company. They paid a hefty punishment for not following data protection standards and had to deal with several patient lawsuits, which cost them a pretty penny.

Good Reasons to Think About Adopting Cybersecurity Strategies

Protecting Your Assets

You can safeguard your important data and systems by investing in cybersecurity. Intellectual property, financial records, and consumer information are all part of this. Secure your company's assets against cybercriminals by lowering the probability of data breaches and other forms of cyberattacks.

Building Customer Trust

When customers know that you take cybersecurity seriously, they are more likely to trust your business with their sensitive information. This trust can lead to increased customer loyalty and positive word-of-mouth, helping you grow your business.

Compliance with Regulations

Businesses have to comply to the varied cybersecurity laws set out by various industries. You can stay out of trouble with the law and make sure you're in compliance with these rules by implementing strong cybersecurity policies.

Minimizing Downtime

Significant downtime, affecting your company operations, can be caused by cyber-attacks. You may lessen the blow to your company's bottom line in the event of an attack by preparing for it ahead of time with a solid cybersecurity plan.

Staying Competitive

Failure to invest in cybersecurity might put firms at a disadvantage as cyber threats grow. You can keep ahead of the competition in your sector by being proactive and using the most recent security measures.

Peace of Mind

A sense of security for your company against cyber attacks is reassuring. Without being preoccupied with the possibility of cyberattacks, you are free to concentrate on operating and expanding your organization.

If you want to keep your company safe from cybercriminals, you need to learn the ropes of cybersecurity. The best way to protect your small business against typical cyberattacks like phishing, ransomware, and malware is to educate yourself on the subject. In addition to safeguarding assets, implementing robust cybersecurity measures enhances consumer confidence, guarantees regulatory compliance, reduces downtime, maintains competitiveness, and offers tranquility. Putting money into cybersecurity is essential in this digital age; it's also a good business move.

Chapter 3: Getting Started with Cybersecurity

Assessing Your Risks

Recognizing the threats your company faces is the initial step in implementing a cybersecurity strategy. Finding out what sensitive information you must safeguard and how it could be at danger is the first step in doing a risk assessment. Examining the store's physical location, its points of access, and any weaknesses in its defenses is analogous to this procedure.

Case in point: Put yourself in the shoes of a small-town store owner. Your sales database, personnel records, and customers' credit card details are all significant pieces of information. When you're doing a risk assessment, you should think about all the ways this information may get out, such a phishing email or a software flaw.

You may conduct a cybersecurity audit to evaluate your risks. Finding any holes in your present security procedures is part of this process. A simple audit can be performed as follows:

1. Identify Your Assets: Make a list of all the digital assets that need protection. This

includes computers, servers, mobile devices, software applications, and data.

2. Evaluate Threats: Identify potential threats to these assets. Common threats include malware, phishing attacks, insider threats, and physical theft.

3. Analyze Vulnerabilities: Determine where your assets are vulnerable. This could be due to outdated software, weak passwords, or lack of employee training.

4. Assess Impact: Consider the potential impact of each threat on your business. For example, a data breach could result in financial loss and damage to your reputation.

5. Implement Controls: Put in place measures to mitigate these risks. This might include updating software, training employees, and using strong passwords.

Educating Your Team

Educating your staff should be your next step after identifying potential dangers. In the fight against cybercrime, your staff should be your first line of protection. Their vulnerability to cyberattacks can be greatly diminished if you teach them the fundamentals of cybersecurity.

Give an overview of typical cyber risks and their potential occurrences. Make sure everyone understands by using plain, non-technical language.

As an example, you may describe phishing emails as malicious attempts to acquire critical information using deceptive email communications that seem official.

So, you run a little legal practice. Training your personnel on a regular basis can help them spot phishing emails and identify malicious links and attachments. Remind them that they should always check the sender's identity before clicking on any links in unsolicited emails.

Steps to Educate Your Team:

1. Regular Training Sessions: Schedule regular cybersecurity training sessions. Use real-life examples to illustrate common threats.
2. Phishing Simulations: Conduct phishing simulations to test your employees' ability to recognize and respond to phishing attempts.
3. Clear Policies: Make sure your cybersecurity policies are crystal clear and that all staff are aware of and abide by them. Password policies, device policies, and data handling policies are all part of this.

4. Accessible Resources: Provide resources such as guides and videos that employees can refer to for information on cybersecurity best practices.

Implementing Strong Passwords and Two-Factor Authentication

Using robust passwords and two-factor authentication (2FA) is a simple and effective solution to safeguard your data. Hackers have a hard time guessing strong passwords because they are lengthy and unique combinations of letters, numbers, and symbols.

Just to give you an idea, if your password is "password123," it's almost hacker heaven. Passwords such as "G7h!Pq#4Vz" are more secure. Look into getting a password manager if you're having trouble coming up with secure passwords to use. Notable password managers in the industry include LastPass, 1Password, and the free alternative, Bitwarden.

A second piece of identity, in addition to your password, is required with two-factor authentication, which increases the security level. A fingerprint scan or a code texted to your phone might be used for this. This additional layer of security ensures that your account remains secure, even in the event that a hacker manages to steal your password.

An actual example would be entering your password in order to access your email account. The next step is to input the code that was delivered to your phone. No one will be able to access your email even if they know your password because of this feature.

Steps to Implement Strong Passwords and 2FA:

1. Password Policies: Create policies that require strong, unique passwords for all accounts. Avoid common words and use a mix of characters.

2. Password Managers: Encourage employees to use password managers to generate and store complex passwords securely. Examples include LastPass, 1Password, and Bitwarden.

3. Enable 2FA: Set up two-factor authentication for all critical accounts. Most major services, like Google, Microsoft, and Apple, offer 2FA options.

Keeping Software Up to Date

In order to obtain access to systems, cybercriminals frequently use weaknesses in out-of-date software. One easy and effective thing you can do to safeguard your company against these kinds of assaults is to always use the most recent version of software. Updates to software frequently contain fixes for newly found security flaws.

Old versions of accounting software may include security holes that cybercriminals are aware of and may take advantage of. These vulnerabilities have been resolved in the newest version. Make sure you update to the latest version.

Many software programs offer automatic updates, which can save you time and ensure your systems are always protected. Make sure to enable this feature whenever possible.

Steps to Keep Software Up to Date:
1. Enable Automatic Updates: For all operating systems (Windows, Mac, Linux) and software applications, enable automatic updates to ensure you always have the latest security patches.
2. Regular Checks: Regularly check for updates for software that does not support automatic updates.
3. Inventory Software: Maintain an inventory of all software used in your business to ensure nothing is overlooked during updates.

Backing Up Your Data

When you back up your data, you make a copy of all of your critical files and put them somewhere safe. That way, you can swiftly recover your data in the event that it is lost, stolen, or compromised. If you want to keep downtime and data loss to a minimum, you must back up your data regularly.

Imagine all of your company's data is encrypted by a ransomware assault. Your data can be restored without paying the ransom if you back it up regularly. Backups may be set to happen automatically with many cloud storage providers. Look at open-source software like Duplicati if you're looking for a free option.

Steps to Back Up Your Data:
1. Identify Critical Data: Determine which data is essential to your business operations and prioritize its backup.
2. Choose a Backup Solution: Select a backup solution that fits your needs. Cloud storage services like Google Drive, Dropbox, and OneDrive are user-friendly and offer automatic backups. For more control, consider using open-source software like Duplicati.
3. Set a Backup Schedule: Regularly back up your data, ideally daily. Automatic backup settings can simplify this process.
4. Test Backups: Periodically test your backups to ensure that data can be successfully restored.

Setting Up Firewalls and Antivirus Software

Firewalls prevent unwanted users from accessing your network while allowing permitted traffic to get through. By scanning your computers for known malware, antivirus software eliminates it.

A firewall acts as a security guard at a building's door, screening incoming visitors to ensure only authorized individuals are allowed entry. Similar to a health inspector, antivirus software is always on the lookout for infections and takes swift action when detected.

Firewalls and Antivirus Options by OS:

1. Windows:
    - Firewall: Windows Defender Firewall is built into Windows and provides basic protection. For more robust options, consider third-party solutions like Norton or McAfee.
    - Antivirus: Windows Defender Antivirus comes pre-installed and offers good protection. Alternatives include Avast, AVG, and Bitdefender.
2. Mac:
    - Firewall: macOS has a built-in firewall that can be enabled in System Preferences. For enhanced protection, consider third-party firewalls like Little Snitch or Intego NetBarrier.
    - Antivirus: macOS does not come with built-in antivirus software. Recommended options include Avast, Sophos, and Norton.
3. Linux:
    - Firewall: Linux users can use iptables or ufw (Uncomplicated Firewall) for firewall protection. For more user-friendly options, consider using GUFW.
    - Antivirus: ClamAV is a popular free antivirus solution for Linux. For more

comprehensive protection, consider using Sophos or Bitdefender.

Steps to Set Up Firewalls and Antivirus Software:

1. Enable Built-In Firewalls: Ensure that the built-in firewall on your operating system is enabled and properly configured.
2. Install Antivirus Software: Choose an antivirus solution that fits your needs and install it on all devices. Ensure that it is set to update automatically.
3. Regular Scans: Schedule regular scans with your antivirus software to detect and remove malware.
4. Monitor Firewall Logs: Regularly review your firewall logs to identify and respond to any suspicious activity.

Beginning a cybersecurity program requires a risk assessment, team education, strong passwords, two-factor authentication, software updates, data backups, firewalls, and antivirus software. Following these procedures will keep your company safe from cybercriminals and keep your data and systems protected. By using these tactics, you may protect your assets, gain consumer confidence, stay compliant, minimize downtime, stay competitive, and have peace of mind. In today's digital age, investing in cybersecurity is a must.

Chapter 4: Developing a Cybersecurity Policy

Importance of a Cybersecurity Policy

Your company's data and IT assets can be better protected from cybercriminals by following a cybersecurity policy. Imagine it as a set of guidelines that all employees in your company must follow in order to be safe when using the internet. A well-defined cybersecurity policy is critical for several reasons.

First and foremost, it makes sure that everyone in your company knows what they should be doing to keep confidential information safe. By having clear expectations, employees are more inclined to adhere to best practices, such as creating robust passwords and being wary of phishing communications. By working together, we can greatly lessen the likelihood of cyberattacks.

Picture yourself as the boss of a tiny advertising firm. Each employee may handle customer data differently in the absence of a cybersecurity policy. Some people may save critical information on an insecure personal device, while others may use a basic password for their email. Data breaches would be less likely if a cybersecurity policy was in place and everyone used safe devices and strong passwords.

Second, having a cybersecurity policy in place ensures that your company follows all applicable laws and regulations. A number of sectors have enacted data protection laws, such as the EU's General Data Protection Regulation (GDPR) and the California Consumer Privacy Act (CCPA). To protect your company from penalties and legal trouble, make sure your policy is well-written and covers all the bases.

Last but not least, a cybersecurity policy may do wonders for your company's credibility. Businesses that value their customers' and clients' privacy are more likely to earn their trust. According to a poll, over 90% of customers would go elsewhere to conduct business if they had doubts about a company's commitment to responsible data handling. Your dedication to cybersecurity will go a long way toward earning your clients' confidence and loyalty.

Key Elements of a Cybersecurity Policy

A comprehensive cybersecurity policy should cover several key elements to effectively protect your business. Here are the main components you should include:

Purpose and Scope

Establishing the policy's goals and boundaries should be the first steps. Please clarify who this policy is intended to protect and why cybersecurity is crucial. Make sure everyone knows how important this part is by reading it first. It sets the tone for the whole work.

The purpose of this cybersecurity policy is to ensure that all of our company's data is secure, private, and accessible at all times. Anyone with access to our system or data, including employees, independent contractors, and business partners, is subject to this.

Roles and Responsibilities

Clearly define the functions and duties of each individual contributing to the upkeep of cybersecurity. Everyone from normal employees to management and IT are part of this. It is everyone's responsibility to assist keep the company's info secure.

Example: "All employees are responsible for safeguarding their login credentials and reporting any suspicious activities. The IT department is responsible for maintaining security software and hardware, conducting regular audits, and responding to security incidents."

Acceptable Use Policy

Make sure everyone's roles and responsibilities related to cybersecurity are defined. This includes everyone from regular workers to upper management and IT. Helping to keep the company's information safe is everyone's job.

Example: "Employees must use company email accounts for work-related communication only. Personal use of company computers should be kept to a minimum and should not involve visiting potentially harmful websites."

Password Management

Give instructions on how to make and keep track of passwords. Keep in mind that you should always use a different, strong password and change them frequently. You might want to think about suggesting that your staff utilize password managers so they can safely store and retrieve their credentials.

Example: "Passwords must be at least ten characters long and include a mix of letters, numbers, and special characters. Employees should change their passwords every 90 days and should not reuse passwords for multiple accounts."

Data Protection and Encryption

Outline the proper procedures for handling and safeguarding sensitive information. Instructions for encrypting data while it is in motion and at rest are part of this. Data encryption makes it impossible to decipher, even if someone were to intercept it, without the encryption key.

Example: "All sensitive data, such as customer information and financial records, must be encrypted using industry-standard encryption methods. Data transmitted over the internet must be sent via secure protocols such as HTTPS."

Incident Response

Provide a plan for what to do if a security breach occurs. Finding the breach, limiting the damage, eliminating the danger, and recovering from the incident are all part of this process. If you want to recover quickly after a breach and keep the damage to a minimum, you need an incident response strategy.

Example: "In the event of a security breach, employees must immediately report the incident to the IT department. The IT department will then contain the breach, investigate its cause, and work to restore normal operations as quickly as possible."

Training and Awareness

A program of continuous cybersecurity education and awareness must be prioritized. Ongoing education keeps workers abreast of emerging risks and effective practices. Training should be described in this area along with the planned dates and methods.

Example: "All employees must participate in annual cybersecurity training sessions. Additionally, quarterly updates will be provided to keep everyone informed about new threats and security measures."

Monitoring and Enforcement

Make clear the procedures for checking and enforcing adherence to the cybersecurity policy. As part of this, there will be frequent audits, assessments of performance, and penalties for failing to comply. To have a strong cybersecurity stance, accountability must be ensured.

Example: "The IT department will conduct quarterly audits to ensure compliance with this policy. Employees found in violation of the policy may face disciplinary action, up to and including termination of employment."

Phishing Response

If an employee suspects a phishing effort, they should know what to do. Cybercriminals frequently employ phishing as a means to deceive victims into divulging important information.

Example: "If an employee receives a suspicious email, they should not click on any links or attachments. Instead, they should report the email to the IT department immediately. The IT department will then analyze the email and take appropriate action."

Backup Policy

Specify the procedures for safely backing up and storing data. In the event of a data breach or system failure, it is crucial to have regular backups to restore data.

Example: "All critical data must be backed up daily. Backups should be stored both onsite and offsite to ensure redundancy. Backup data must be encrypted and regularly tested to ensure it can be successfully restored."

How to Create and Enforce a Cybersecurity Policy

Creating and enforcing a cybersecurity policy for your small business involves several steps. Here's a step-by-step guide to help you get started:

Assess Your Needs

Evaluate the unique cybersecurity requirements of your company first. Take into account the data types you manage, the risks you may encounter, and the regulations and laws that apply to you. By doing so, you may customize your policy to meet your specific needs and overcome any obstacles you may face.

Draft the Policy

Create your cybersecurity policy with the help of the essential components mentioned before. To make sure that everyone in your company can comprehend it, keep the language plain and straightforward. Make the policy more approachable by including real-life examples to demonstrate important aspects.

Review and Revise

Once you have a draft, review it with key stakeholders, including IT staff, management, and legal advisors. Their feedback can help you identify any gaps or areas that need clarification. Revise the policy as needed to ensure it is comprehensive and practical.

Communicate the Policy

Make sure that all staff understand the policy. Gather everyone together for a first meeting to go over the policy, why it's important, and how it will influence their work. Make sure that a written copy of the policy is readily available for future reference and provide it to them.

Conduct Training

Assist staff in comprehending and adhering to the policy through training. To make things more interesting for students with varying learning styles, try combining face-to-face meetings with internet resources and articles. Keep training materials current by adding fresh material on emerging dangers and recommended practices.

Monitor Compliance

Use audits and performance reviews to check for policy compliance on a regular basis. Make use of technologies that can monitor actions like data access, incident reports, and password changes. If you do this, you can find problems before they happen and fix them quickly.

Enforce the Policy

Be consistent in your enforcement of the policy to make sure everyone knows it means business. Be fair in your application of the clearly stated consequences for noncompliance. For recurrent infractions, disciplinary action may be necessary, in addition to warnings or extra training.

Review and Update

There is a continual flux between cybersecurity risks and recommended procedures. To keep your policy up-to-date and effective, review it often and make any necessary updates. If you want to make sure the policy is still relevant and helps workers and stakeholders find ways to enhance it, you should ask for their comments.

Using the points made above, below is an example of a small business cybersecurity policy:

XYZ Company Cybersecurity Policy

Purpose and Scope

This cybersecurity policy aims to protect the integrity, confidentiality, and availability of XYZ Company's information assets. It applies to all employees, contractors, and third-party partners who have access to our network and data.

Roles and Responsibilities

- Employees: Safeguard login credentials, report suspicious activities, follow cybersecurity best practices.
- IT Department: Maintain security software and hardware, conduct regular audits, respond to security incidents.
- Management: Support and enforce the cybersecurity policy, ensure adequate resources for cybersecurity measures.

Acceptable Use Policy

- Use company email accounts for work-related communication only.

- Keep personal use of company computers to a minimum; avoid visiting potentially harmful websites.

Password Management

- Passwords must be at least eight characters long and include a mix of letters, numbers, and special characters.
- Change passwords every 90 days; do not reuse passwords for multiple accounts.

Data Protection and Encryption

- Encrypt all sensitive data, such as customer information and financial records.
- Use secure protocols like HTTPS for data transmission over the internet.

Incident Response

- Report security breaches immediately to the IT department.
- The IT department will contain, investigate, and resolve breaches promptly.

Training and Awareness

- Mandatory annual cybersecurity training for all employees.
- Quarterly updates on new threats and security measures.

Monitoring and Enforcement

- Quarterly audits by the IT department to ensure compliance.
- Disciplinary action for policy violations, up to and including termination of employment.

Phishing Response

- If an employee receives a suspicious email, they should not click on any links or attachments.
- Report the email to the IT department immediately for analysis and action.

Backup Policy

- Critical data must be backed up daily.
- Backups should be stored both onsite and offsite to ensure redundancy.
- Backup data must be encrypted and regularly tested to ensure it can be successfully restored.

Chapter 5: Implementing Cybersecurity Measures

Network Security

Keeping your computer network safe from intruders and malicious software is the main goal of network security. Like when you lock your doors and windows and maybe even set up a security system to protect your house, this is only a precautionary measure. To make your network more secure, consider these simple steps:

Network Segmentation

The process of network segmentation is separating a computer network into more manageable pieces. This reduces the likelihood of malware spreading and restricts access to sensitive data. If your network were a huge office building, network segmentation would be the equivalent of establishing restricted areas that only authorized individuals are able to access.

You are the manager of a local medical facility. You can set up network segments so that only medical staff can access patient records and that only office workers may access administrative data. This ensures that private patient data cannot be accessed by an attacker who compromises a single network node.

The potential for extensive harm in the event of a cyberattack can be mitigated by segmentation.

Businesses may limit the scope of a breach to a specific region by implementing network segmentation. This helps to minimize damage and response costs.

Secure Wi-Fi

Protecting your internet connection from unwanted access is the primary goal of a secure Wi-Fi network. When protecting your Wi-Fi, make sure you use strong passwords and encryption.

Case study: You can't go wrong with providing complimentary Wi-Fi as a customer service tool for coffee shops. Unprotected Wi-Fi, on the other hand, leaves your company and your customers' devices vulnerable to hackers. Encrypting your Wi-Fi using WPA3 and a robust password will restrict access to authorized users exclusively.

If you take these precautions, your company's data will be safer, and your consumers will rest easy knowing that their data is too.

Guest Wi-Fi

A guest Wi-Fi network allows customers to use your internet connection without affecting your primary company network. One way for guests to connect to the internet is through a dedicated guest Wi-Fi network.

Imagine you have a small accounting business and that clients drop by your office quite a bit. They may stay online without compromising your important company data by using a guest Wi-Fi network.

Steps to Set Up Guest Wi-Fi:

1. Create a Separate Network: Most modern routers allow you to create a separate guest network. This keeps guest traffic isolated from your main business network.
2. Use a Strong Password: Ensure the guest Wi-Fi network has a strong, unique password. Avoid using the same password as your main network.
3. Enable Network Isolation: Many routers have a feature that prevents devices on the guest network from communicating with each other or with devices on the main network. Enable this feature to enhance security.
4. Limit Bandwidth: To prevent guests from using too much of your internet bandwidth, set a bandwidth limit on the guest network. This ensures your business operations aren't affected by heavy guest usage.

5. Monitor Network Activity: Regularly monitor the guest network for any unusual activity. This can help you quickly identify and respond to potential security threats.

Benefits of Guest Wi-Fi:

1. Enhanced Security: By isolating guest traffic, you protect your main network from potential threats brought in by guest devices.
2. Improved Performance: Limiting bandwidth on the guest network ensures that your main business operations have sufficient internet resources.
3. Professionalism: Offering guest Wi-Fi shows that you care about your visitors' convenience and security, enhancing your business's professionalism and customer service.

Device Security

The primary goal of device security is to prevent unauthorized access to specific electronic devices. The gadgets that store and process your company's data are just as important as the expensive possessions you keep in your house.

Device Encryption

When data is encrypted on a device, it becomes a code that only authorized users can decipher. Putting your documents in a safe is the same as doing this. No one can access the data, even if the device is stolen, because only the owner of the encryption key has it.

Case in point: Suppose you were traveling and your laptop went missing. If your laptop is encrypted, a burglar will need the password to access any sensitive company emails or customer data. As a result, there is less chance of sensitive information falling into the wrong hands.

Data breaches are drastically reduced for businesses that encrypt their devices. Your business can avoid possible financial and brand harm by taking one easy step.

Endpoint Protection

The goal of endpoint protection is to prevent viruses and cyberattacks on specific devices. It's the same as setting up home security systems with cameras and alarms to monitor for and stop unwanted visitors.

Imagine that members of your marketing team utilize a variety of devices to access internal corporate information. You can safeguard your devices against malware and hacking attempts by installing firewalls and antivirus software on each one.

Antivirus, firewall, and anti-phishing capabilities are common elements of endpoint protection software, which offers full security for all of your devices.

Access Controls

Access controls determine who can access your data and systems. It's like having a keycard system in an office building, where only authorized personnel can enter certain areas. Proper access controls help prevent unauthorized access and reduce the risk of insider threats.

Role-Based Access Control (RBAC)

Role-based access control assigns permissions based on an employee's role within the organization. This ensures that individuals only have access to the information necessary for their job. It's like giving keys to different rooms in a building only to those who need them.

For a small store, the point-of-sale system may be all that's needed for cashiers, while supervisors may obtain statistics on sales and inventory.

Restrict Access Control (RBAC) helps to prevent data breaches by limiting employee access to only the information they require.

Data leaks and security breaches can be better mitigated when RBAC is used by businesses.

Multi-Factor Authentication (MFA)

Two or more verification methods are required to access an account using multi-factor authentication, which provides an additional layer of protection.

Example from real life: In order to access your company email, you must first input your password. After that, you'll need to input the code that you got on your phone in order to finish logging in. Your account remains secure even if someone manages to obtain your password since they will need the code that was given to your phone.

The likelihood of unwanted access is much diminished with MFA. The likelihood of a hack occurring in an account that uses MFA rather than just a password is significantly lower.

Data Protection

Protecting your company's data against loss, misuse, or alteration is what data protection is all about. This safeguards sensitive information and guarantees its exclusive utilization for its designated purpose.

Data Classification

Data classification is sorting information into different buckets according to how sensitive and important it is. Picture this: you have a folder for public materials, another for sensitive documents, and a third for top secret documents.

Case in point: Marketing materials are made public in a small law office, but client agreements and legal papers are considered secret. As a result, sensitive information is protected to an adequate degree.

Companies may better secure sensitive information and meet legal requirements by using data categorization.

Data Loss Prevention (DLP)

Data loss prevention tools aid in keeping confidential information within the company. It's quite similar to setting up a home security system that notifies you if someone attempts to take your important possessions.

Case in point: A data loss prevention system can notify IT if an employee attempts to send sensitive customer lists to their personal email. Data leaks, whether unintentional or purposeful, are prevented by this.

In order to keep their clients' and customers' confidence and prevent expensive data breaches, firms should use DLP technologies.

Protecting your company's data, devices, networks, and access points with these cybersecurity steps may make a world of difference. Your company's data and systems will be protected from cybercriminals if you follow these procedures.

In addition to protecting your assets, these measures will earn your customers' trust, ease your compliance with regulations, and calm your nerves. For small firms, these cybersecurity precautions are both practical and cost-effective, which is essential in today's digital environment.

Chapter 6: Monitoring and Responding to Cyber Threats

Importance of Continuous Monitoring

Because it enables companies to identify and react to threats instantly, continuous monitoring is crucial in cybersecurity. Imagine it as having a personal security guard who is on the lookout for any unusual behavior at all times. Problems can be caught before they escalate if you constantly monitor your network and systems.

Continuous monitoring helps in several ways:

1. Early Detection: Unusual network behavior might be caught in the nick of time with constant network monitoring. You may react swiftly and stop more damage with this early detection. Take continuous monitoring as an example. It may tell you instantly if a hacker attempts to enter your network, giving you the opportunity to take action before any data is stolen.

2. Minimizing Damage: In order to minimize damage, it is important to discover threats early so that they may be contained swiftly. Preventing data breaches and costly downtime is possible with this. Companies may mitigate losses by as much as 70% if they identify and

react to security risks within the first twenty-four hours.

3. Compliance: To ensure compliance, certain sectors have rules that call for constant vigilance over all systems and networks. To prevent penalties and legal trouble, make sure your company follows all the rules by using constant monitoring.

4. Building Trust: Consumers are more inclined to have faith in a company that prioritizes cybersecurity. Your reputation and client loyalty may be boosted by constantly monitoring your network. This shows that you are committed to protecting your customers' data.

Tools and Techniques for Monitoring

You can keep a constant eye on your network and systems with the help of a number of tools and methods. Listed here are a handful of the best:

SIEM (Security Information and Event Management)

In order to find security risks, SIEM solutions gather and analyze data from all across your network. They analyze security alarms produced by apps and network hardware in real-time. To further understand what SIEM is, it's helpful to think of it as a sophisticated security system that keeps tabs on your company's operations and sounds an alert if anything out of the ordinary is spotted.

Say you're in charge of an online store. Your website's traffic and user activity may be monitored with a SIEM solution. It can notify you of a possible brute force assault if it notices an abrupt spike in login attempts from various IP addresses, giving you the opportunity to act promptly.

Freeware Options:

- AlienVault OSSIM: This open-source SIEM tool integrates multiple security monitoring functions into a single platform, making it accessible and useful for small businesses.
- Wazuh: open-source security platform designed for threat detection and incident response.

Alternatives for Windows and Mac:

- Windows:
  - Graylog: An open-source log management tool that can be used for SIEM purposes, offering powerful log analysis features.
  - Splunk Free: A free version of Splunk, suitable for small businesses with limited data volumes.

- Mac:
    - LogRhythm NetMon Freemium: Provides network monitoring and forensic capabilities and can be used on macOS.
    - Splunk Free: Also available for Mac, providing robust log management and analysis capabilities.

Which Companies Can Benefit from SIEM?

Using SIEM technologies should be considered by small firms that handle sensitive data, whether it's financial information, healthcare records, or massive amounts of client data. Companies that are subject to stringent regulatory compliance, e-commerce sites, healthcare providers, and financial institutions are the ones that profit the most from SIEM solutions.

Intrusion Detection Systems (IDS)

Network traffic is monitored by intrusion detection systems for any signs of known or unusual activities. In the event that someone attempts to break into your house, they will alert you, much like a burglar alarm. Two primary varieties of intrusion detection systems are host-based and network-based.

Intrusion Detection Systems (IDS) that are network-based (NIDS): These systems check all network traffic for any signs of malicious behavior. Having it pointed at your building's main entrance is like having a security camera.

Host-based intrusion detection systems (HIDS) keep tabs on what's happening on a single server or device. It's the same as installing a motion detector in your building; it will notify you if somebody moves in without your permission.

An actual-life example would be the employment of network intrusion detection systems (NIDS) by a small financial business owner to keep tabs on client and server activity. If the intrusion detection system notices suspicious traffic patterns, including a high volume of data moved at inconvenient times, it might notify you of a possible data breach.

Freeware Options:

- Snort: A popular open-source network-based IDS that can detect various types of network attacks and provide real-time alerts.
- Suricata: Another open-source network IDS, Suricata offers high performance and extensive protocol support.

Alternatives for Windows and Mac:

- Windows:
    - Security Onion: A free and open-source Linux distribution for intrusion detection, network security monitoring,

and log management, which can be run on a Windows-based network.
- ○ OSSEC: An open-source HIDS that provides detailed logging, file integrity checking, and rootkit detection, compatible with Windows.
- Mac:
  - ○ OSSEC: Also compatible with macOS, providing comprehensive host-based intrusion detection.
  - ○ Snorby: A web-based interface for Snort, making it easier to manage and review alerts on macOS.

Which Businesses Should Use IDS?

Implementing IDS is a must for businesses that handle regulated or sensitive data, including online merchants, healthcare providers, and financial institutions. Internal detection systems are useful for all types of businesses, but especially for those with a wide variety of networks or those that are vulnerable to targeted attacks.

In order to identify and react to attacks faster, intrusion detection systems might be useful. Companies that use intrusion detection systems see a marked decrease in successful cyber-attacks. This is because these systems offer another line of protection against hackers.

Incident Response Planning

To better prepare your company to identify, contain, and recover from cyber disasters, it is a good idea to create an incident response strategy. This document lays out the steps your company will take in the event of an emergency, such as a fire or natural catastrophe. Reducing the damage from a cyberattack and getting back up and running quickly are both made easier with a clearly laid out incident response strategy.

Creating a Response Plan

Creating an effective incident response plan involves several steps:

1. Identify Potential Threats: List the types of cyber threats your business might face, such as phishing, ransomware, and insider threats. Understanding these threats will help you prepare appropriate responses.

2. Establish Response Procedures: Define the steps to be taken when an incident occurs. This includes identifying the incident, containing the damage, eradicating the threat, and recovering from the incident. Make sure the procedures are clear and easy to follow.

3. Assign Roles and Responsibilities: Designate specific roles and responsibilities for your incident response team. This ensures that everyone knows what to do during an incident,

reducing confusion and improving response time.

4. Develop Communication Plans: Create a plan for communicating with employees, customers, and other stakeholders during and after an incident. Transparency is key to maintaining trust and minimizing panic.

5. Regularly Update the Plan: Cyber threats are constantly evolving, so it's important to regularly review and update your incident response plan to address new threats and changes in your business operations.

As an actual example, let's say you're the manager of a little medical facility. For example, in the event of a ransomware attack, your incident response plan may outline how you detect and contain the infection, inform impacted patients, and restore data from backups.

Establishing a Response Team

A team of people tasked with handling and reacting to cyber problems is known as an incident response team. To guarantee a thorough response, this team should incorporate personnel from all departments.

Key roles in the incident response team include:

- Incident Coordinator: Oversees the response effort and ensures that all procedures are followed.

- IT Security Specialist: Identifies and analyzes the incident, implements technical responses, and restores affected systems.
- Communications Officer: Manages internal and external communications, including notifying affected parties and handling media inquiries.
- Legal Advisor: Ensures that the response complies with legal and regulatory requirements and provides guidance on legal implications.

In the event of a data breach at your small business, for instance, the following roles would be activated: incident coordinator, IT security specialist, communications officer, and legal advisor. The former two would deal with informing employees and customers, while the latter two would handle notifying regulators.

Conducting Post-Incident Reviews

Doing a post-incident review after dealing with a cybersecurity event will help you understand what went wrong and how to fix it next time. If you want to know how to avoid future occurrences like this one, this evaluation will show you where your incident response strategy is strong and where it needs improvement.

Steps to Conduct a Post-Incident Review:

1. Document the Incident: Record all details of the incident, including the timeline of events, the nature of the threat, and the actions taken. This documentation is essential for analyzing the incident and improving your response plan.
2. Analyze the Incident: Review the incident to determine how it occurred, what vulnerabilities were exploited, and what impact it had on your business. This analysis helps identify areas for improvement in your security measures and response procedures.
3. Gather Feedback: Collect feedback from all members of the incident response team and other affected parties. This feedback provides valuable insights into what worked well and what could be improved.
4. Update the Response Plan: Based on the findings from the review, update your incident response plan to address any identified weaknesses and incorporate lessons learned. This ensures that your plan evolves with the changing threat landscape.
5. Implement Preventive Measures: Take steps to address the vulnerabilities identified during the review. This might include updating software, enhancing security training for employees, or implementing additional security measures.

Conducting a post-incident analysis after a phishing attempt on your small firm reveals that many workers clicked on a fraudulent link. This new information informs your response strategy, which now calls for more stringent email filtering rules and more thorough phishing awareness training.

As part of any thorough cybersecurity plan, monitoring for cyber threats and taking action when necessary are essential. You can defend your company from cyber dangers and guarantee a quick recovery when events happen if you execute continuous monitoring, use technologies like SIEM and IDS, make an efficient plan for responding to occurrences, and do evaluations thereafter.

In addition to protecting your company's assets, these investments will earn your customers' trust, ease your legal compliance burden, and calm your nerves. To safeguard your company's data and systems against cyber attacks, build a strong cybersecurity framework according to the procedures given in this chapter.

These techniques are essential for small businesses to thrive in today's digital age. They are practical and cost-effective. Your company can remain operational and secure from cyber attacks if you take preventative measures and are well-prepared.

Chapter 7: Building a Cybersecurity Culture

Making Cybersecurity a Part of Everyday Operations

The best way to build a cybersecurity culture is to make security a part of your company's daily routine. Employees should develop cybersecurity habits similar to how wearing a seatbelt is already standard operating procedure. Making ensuring everyone is on the same page regarding the significance of security and their part in keeping the business safe is part of this.

The foundation of a robust cybersecurity culture is good leadership. The rest of the company follows the example set by executives who make cybersecurity a priority and act responsibly. For instance, it's more probable that staff will use difficult passwords and multi-factor authentication if the CEO does.

Integrating security checks into normal procedures is a straightforward method to integrate cybersecurity into daily operations. Employees should check the addresses of those who will be receiving critical emails and, if needed, encrypt the messages before sending them. Secure your data and emails with ease with shareware like VeraCrypt. It works with both Mac and Windows computers.

Put yourself in the shoes of an advertising agency owner. Data belonging to clients and private ideas are integral to every project. Your team can safeguard sensitive customer data and IP by regularly utilizing encrypted email and secure file storage. Workers are less prone to make security blunders when they perceive these procedures as routine in their work.

According to statistics, fewer breaches occur at firms that have a strong culture of cybersecurity. Employees are more likely to adhere to security measures and are also more cognizant of potential dangers. Many security mishaps are caused by human mistake; a robust culture reduces this.

Training and Awareness Programs

Establishing a culture of cybersecurity relies heavily on training and awareness initiatives. By attending training on a regular basis, staff may learn about new risks and best practices. Additionally, it emphasizes the significance of cybersecurity in their everyday tasks.

Practical and interesting training is ideal. To better understand typical dangers such as phishing and ransomware, it is helpful to look at real-life examples. When workers can perceive how new information is relevant to their job, they are more inclined to retain and use that information. As an example, you may train your staff to see and react appropriately to phishing emails by simulating such assaults.

Freeware training tools:

- Phishing Simulators: Tools like PhishMe Free and Cofense PhishMe offer free phishing simulation and training services to help employees recognize and report phishing attempts.
- Cybersecurity Awareness Training: Websites like Cybrary provide free courses on various cybersecurity topics, suitable for both beginners and experienced users.

An actual example would be the use of a phishing simulator in routine training sessions for the owner of a small accounting business. You may find out where your team is falling short and where they are excelling by sending them simulated phishing emails and analyzing their replies. With practice, your staff will be able to recognize and prevent legitimate phishing efforts.

Combining online courses with in-person seminars and interactive activities can increase the effectiveness of training. The information is kept fresh and different learning styles are catered to in this way. Training materials should be updated on a regular basis to keep personnel up-to-date on security risks and procedures.

Encouraging Open Communication About Cybersecurity

In order to have a robust cybersecurity culture, open communication is essential. Everyone on staff should be allowed to speak freely about security issues and possible dangers. This contributes to a setting where all employees are actively involved in safeguarding the organization.

Motivate your staff to speak up by asking questions and offering feedback. Set up avenues for people to report security concerns, such a specific email address or a way to report them anonymously. Make it simple for workers to report issues and reassuring that their feedback will be considered.

An actual example would be if you were the manager of a small retail establishment and your employees started reporting more questionable emails. Talk about these findings in team meetings instead of dismissing them, and stress how important it is to be vigilant. Motivating other employees to disclose possible dangers requires acknowledging those who do so.

Open communication about cybersecurity helps firms identify and mitigate risks better, according to statistics. The reason behind this is because when employees feel appreciated for their opinion, they are more inclined to report suspicious conduct and adhere to security rules.

Celebrating Successes and Learning from Failures

Good cybersecurity practices may be reinforced by acknowledging and rewarding victories. Recognize and reward staff when they effectively detect and prevent security vulnerabilities or phishing attempts. Others may be encouraged to maintain vigilance and initiative by this positive reinforcement.

Concurrently, it's critical to gain knowledge from setbacks without pointing fingers. Make the most of security incidents by analyzing them and figuring out how to make your defenses and processes better. Find out what went wrong and how to avoid repeat incidents by conducting post-incident evaluations.

Imagine your small marketing business suffers a data breach because of an inadequate password. Instead than placing blame on the employee, make a point about how important it is to utilize secure passwords and multi-factor authentication. To stop future breaches, you should alter your password policy and give more training.

Steps to Build a Cybersecurity Culture:

1. Leadership Commitment: Leaders should prioritize cybersecurity and model good practices.

2. Integrate Security into Daily Operations: Make cybersecurity a routine part of every task.
3. Regular Training: Conduct practical and engaging training sessions.
4. Open Communication: Encourage employees to report concerns and share observations.
5. Celebrate Successes: Recognize and reward good cybersecurity practices.
6. Learn from Failures: Use incidents as learning opportunities to improve security.

Tools for Training and Awareness:

- Cybersecurity Training Platforms: Cybrary and Khan Academy offer free cybersecurity courses.
- Phishing Simulation Tools: PhishMe Free and Cofense PhishMe help train employees to recognize phishing attempts.
- Security Awareness Content: Websites like StaySafeOnline provide free resources for educating employees about cybersecurity.

Implementing Security Measures:

- Encryption Tools: VeraCrypt is a free encryption software for protecting sensitive data.
- Password Managers: LastPass and Bitwarden offer free versions to help employees manage strong passwords.

- Two-Factor Authentication (2FA): Use Google Authenticator or Duo Mobile, which are free tools that add an extra layer of security to accounts.

Windows and Mac OS Security Tools:

- Windows:
    - Windows Defender: Built-in antivirus and malware protection.
    - BitLocker: Integrated disk encryption tool for protecting data.
    - Windows Firewall: Built-in firewall to protect against unauthorized access.
- Mac OS:
    - FileVault: Built-in disk encryption tool to protect data.
    - XProtect: Integrated malware detection and removal tool.
    - macOS Firewall: Built-in firewall to protect against unauthorized access.

Integrating security into everyday operations, offering regular training and awareness programs, fostering open communication, celebrating triumphs while learning from errors, and building a cybersecurity culture are all necessary steps. A strong cybersecurity culture may shield your company from danger and keep your data and systems secure if you follow these guidelines.

By taking these precautions, you may rest easy knowing that your company's assets are secure, gain the confidence of your customers, and meet all applicable legal requirements. To safeguard your company's data and systems against cyber attacks, establish a robust cybersecurity culture by adhering to the procedures described in this chapter.

These tactics are practical and inexpensive for small companies, and they are essential in today's digital age. To keep your business functioning efficiently and reduce the effect of cyber attacks, it is important to be proactive and prepared.

Chapter 8: Cybersecurity Frameworks and Compliance

The abundance of acronyms and technical words used in cybersecurity frameworks can make them appear complicated and difficult to understand and apply. Nevertheless, these frameworks offer organized instructions that might simplify the process of safeguarding your company's information. Here we will take a look at two important cybersecurity frameworks: ISO/IEC 27001 and the National Institute of Standards and Technology Cybersecurity Framework. We'll walk you through the process of implementing them in your small business after we explain them in simple terms and give you some examples.

Overview of NIST Cybersecurity Framework

Businesses may better manage and decrease cybersecurity risks with the aid of the NIST Cybersecurity Framework, which was designed by the National Institute of Standards and Technology (NIST). Although the name of the framework is quite complex, it is actually very useful and straightforward. It offers a bird's-eye perspective of cybersecurity risk management over an organization's lifespan through five essential functions:

1. Identify: This involves understanding your business environment and identifying critical assets. It's like making a list of all the valuable items in your house and figuring out where they might be vulnerable.
2. Protect: Implement safeguards to secure your assets. This could be as simple as using strong passwords, encrypting data, and keeping software up to date.
3. Detect: Set up systems to identify when a cybersecurity event occurs. Think of this as installing alarms and cameras to catch intruders.
4. Respond: Have a plan for what to do when a cybersecurity incident happens. This is like having a fire drill plan so everyone knows what to do if there's a fire.
5. Recover: Develop strategies to restore any capabilities or services that were impacted by a cybersecurity incident. It's about bouncing back and returning to normal operations as quickly as possible.

So you're the boss of a small online store. With the help of the NIST Framework, you can do things like recognize that your customer database is valuable (Identify), implement robust authentication procedures (Protect), keep an eye on your network for suspicious behavior (Detect), prepare for data breaches (Respond), and restore customer data from backups (Recover).

With the NIST Framework in place, small firms may better manage cybersecurity risks, which in turn reduces the likelihood of successful attacks and speeds up recovery times.

Freeware Tools for Implementing NIST Framework:

- OpenVAS: An open-source vulnerability scanner to help identify security risks.
- Snort: An intrusion detection system to help detect security breaches.
- CIS Controls: A set of free cybersecurity best practices that align with the NIST Framework.

Overview of ISO/IEC 27001

Managing information security in accordance with ISO/IEC 27001 is a global standard. Implementing, maintaining, and enhancing an information security management system (ISMS) are all outlined in this framework. In reality, it's all about taking a methodical approach to protecting your data, despite the complex sounding moniker.

Key components of ISO/IEC 27001 include:

1. Context of the Organization: Understanding the needs and expectations of your stakeholders and defining the scope of your ISMS.

2. Leadership: Ensuring top management is committed to the ISMS, and defining clear roles and responsibilities.
3. Planning: Identifying risks and opportunities, and planning how to address them.
4. Support: Ensuring adequate resources, awareness, and communication for the ISMS.
5. Operation: Implementing security measures and managing processes to achieve ISMS objectives.
6. Performance Evaluation: Monitoring, measuring, analyzing, and evaluating the ISMS.
7. Improvement: Continually improving the ISMS based on monitoring and review.

You are the manager of a local medical facility. Using ISO/IEC 27001, your ISMS can be defined to include patient records (Context), with management team support (Leadership), risks (Planning) identified, resources (Support) allocated, procedures (Operation) for secure patient data handling put in place, performance (Evaluation) reviewed regularly, and improvements (Improvement) made based on lessons learned.

By implementing ISO/IEC 27001, small firms may safeguard their information assets thoroughly, which improves consumer confidence and helps them stay in line with regulations.

Freeware Tool for Implementing ISO/IEC 27001:

- AuditScripts: Provides free templates and checklists to help implement ISO/IEC 27001.

How to Implement These Frameworks

Though it may appear overwhelming at first, the NIST and ISO/IEC frameworks may be broken down into simple phases for implementation. A starting point for your journey is this guide:

1. Understand Your Needs: Assess your business environment, identify key assets, and understand your specific cybersecurity needs.
2. Choose a Framework: Decide whether NIST, ISO/IEC 27001, or a combination of both best fits your business needs.
3. Define Scope and Objectives: Clearly define the scope of your cybersecurity efforts and set achievable objectives.
4. Develop Policies and Procedures: Create policies and procedures based on the chosen framework. Use templates and guides to simplify this process.
5. Allocate Resources: Ensure you have the necessary resources, including personnel, tools, and training, to implement your cybersecurity plan.
6. Implement Controls: Put in place the necessary technical and organizational measures to protect your assets.

7. Monitor and Review: Continuously monitor your systems, review the effectiveness of your controls, and make improvements as needed.

Beginning with an assessment of their cybersecurity needs, a small software development company can choose to implement the NIST Framework. Then, they can define their scope to include customer data and proprietary code. Next, they can develop policies and procedures for data handling and access control. Then, they can allocate resources for training and security tools. Finally, they can implement controls, such as encryption and routinely review security logs and conduct audits.

Ensuring Compliance with Legal and Regulatory Requirements

Every company must adhere to all applicable laws and regulations. What this means is that you have to follow all the rules and regulations that are in place to keep your data safe. Serious consequences, including penalties, lawsuits, and harm to your credibility, may follow from noncompliance.

Key Compliance Requirements:

1. GDPR (General Data Protection Regulation): Applies to businesses that handle personal data of EU citizens. Requires strict data protection measures and grants individuals rights over their data.

2. HIPAA (Health Insurance Portability and Accountability Act): Applies to healthcare providers in the U.S. and mandates the protection of patient health information.
3. CCPA (California Consumer Privacy Act): Grants California residents rights over their personal data and requires businesses to implement data protection measures.

You are obligated to adhere to GDPR if you own an online store that caters to consumers residing in the EU. Things like getting customers' permission before collecting their data, making it easy for them to see and remove their data, and reporting data breaches to the proper authorities within 72 hours are all part of what this implies.

Steps to Ensure Compliance:

1. Identify Applicable Regulations: Determine which regulations apply to your business based on your industry, location, and the nature of your data.
2. Understand Requirements: Thoroughly review the requirements of the applicable regulations.
3. Develop Compliance Plan: Create a plan to address each requirement. Use templates and guides to simplify the process.
4. Implement Controls: Put in place the necessary technical and organizational measures to achieve compliance.

5. Train Employees: Ensure all employees understand the regulations and their role in maintaining compliance.
6. Monitor and Audit: Regularly monitor your compliance status and conduct audits to identify and address any gaps.

Freeware Tools for Compliance:

- GDPR Compliance Tools: GDPR Toolkit offers free resources and templates for GDPR compliance.
- HIPAA Compliance Tools: HIPAA Journal provides free guides and resources for healthcare providers.
- CCPA Compliance Tools: CCPA Compliance Checklist offers free checklists and templates for businesses.

Windows and Mac OS Security Tools:

- Windows:
  - Windows Defender: Built-in antivirus and malware protection.
  - BitLocker: Integrated disk encryption tool for protecting data.
  - Windows Firewall: Built-in firewall to protect against unauthorized access.
- Mac OS:
  - FileVault: Built-in disk encryption tool to protect data.

- XProtect: Integrated malware detection and removal tool.
- macOS Firewall: Built-in firewall to protect against unauthorized access.

Developing a Solid Cybersecurity Culture

The best way to build a cybersecurity culture is to make security a part of your company's daily routine. Employees should develop cybersecurity habits similar to how wearing a seatbelt is already standard operating procedure. Making ensuring everyone is on the same page regarding the significance of security and their part in keeping the business safe is part of this.

Case in point: Put yourself in the shoes of an advertising agency owner. Data belonging to clients and private ideas are integral to every project. Your team can safeguard sensitive customer data and Intellectual Property by regularly utilizing encrypted email and secure file storage. Workers are less prone to make security blunders when they perceive these procedures as routine in their work.

Steps to Build a Cybersecurity Culture:

1. Leadership Commitment: Leaders should prioritize cybersecurity and model good practices.
2. Integrate Security into Daily Operations: Make cybersecurity a routine part of every task.

3. Regular Training: Conduct practical and engaging training sessions.
4. Open Communication: Encourage employees to report concerns and share observations.
5. Celebrate Successes: Recognize and reward good cybersecurity practices.
6. Learn from Failures: Use incidents as learning opportunities to improve security.

Tools for Training and Awareness:

- Cybersecurity Training Platforms: Cybrary and Khan Academy offer free cybersecurity courses.
- Phishing Simulation Tools: PhishMe Free and Cofense PhishMe help train employees to recognize phishing attempts.
- Security Awareness Content: Websites like StaySafeOnline provide free resources for educating employees about cybersecurity.

Implementing Security Measures:

- Encryption Tools: VeraCrypt is a free encryption software for protecting sensitive data.
- Password Managers: LastPass and Bitwarden offer free versions to help employees manage strong passwords.
- Two-Factor Authentication (2FA): Use Google Authenticator or Duo Mobile, which are tools that add an extra layer of security to accounts.

Your company's security may be greatly improved by learning about and applying cybersecurity frameworks such as NIST and ISO/IEC 27001. These frameworks offer a systematic way to manage and decrease cybersecurity risk, even if they may appear complicated.

If you want to construct a strong cybersecurity culture, incorporate these frameworks into your company operations, and stay in compliance with all applicable laws and regulations, this chapter is for you. Your investments will be safe, your consumers will have faith in you, and you will have peace of mind.

These tactics are practical and inexpensive for small companies, and they are essential in today's digital age. To keep your business functioning efficiently and reduce the effect of cyber attacks, it is important to be proactive and prepared.

Chapter 9: Future-Proofing Your Cybersecurity Strategy

Keeping ahead of cybersecurity risks is essential for every organization in today's fast-paced digital environment. What was effective yesterday may not be tomorrow due to new dangers and technology. In this chapter, we'll look at how to make your cybersecurity plan more resilient to new threats by keeping up with the latest developments, being flexible, investing in your own education, and teaming up with professionals.

Emerging Threats and Technologies

New kinds of cyberattacks appear on a regular basis, and cyber dangers are dynamic in nature. Keep an eye out for these emerging dangers and technologies:

Ransomware: Malware that encrypts your data and then demands payment to decrypt them is known as ransomware. The situation is analogous to having all of your important documents locked away and demanded payment to unlock them. Due to their often laxer security procedures, small businesses are becoming more and more targets of cybercriminals.

A tiny accounting business was attacked by ransomware, as an example from real life. In order to decrypt their encrypted customer records, they were had to pay a substantial amount. Strong backup methods and defense against ransomware were highlighted by this occurrence.

Phishing: Attackers using phishing techniques pose as legitimate businesses or organizations in an effort to deceive victims into divulging critical information. To steal your account information, it's like a con artist pretending to be a bank employee.

Case in point: Upon receiving an email that appeared to have originated from their bank, an employee of a small retail company was requested to verify their login credentials. The worker gave in, and the business lost access to its bank account. This shows how critical it is to teach workers to spot phishing emails.

Internet of Things (IoT) Vulnerabilities: IoT Businesses are increasingly utilizing Internet of Things (IoT) technologies, such as smart thermostats and security cameras. On the other hand, without adequate protection, they can be hacked. It would be the same as if you had several unlocked doors leading into your house.

Example from real life: A little café installed smart cameras to keep customers safe, but nobody ever bothered to reset the factory-set passwords. The café was under constant surveillance because hackers had gained access to the cameras. Strong, unique passwords should be used to safeguard Internet of Things devices, as this event has shown.

Adapting to the Evolving Cybersecurity Landscape

Cybersecurity strategies need to be proactive and adaptable if companies are to stay up with the ever-shifting threat landscape. This is how you can adapt:

1. Regular Updates and Patching: Ensure all software and systems are regularly updated to fix security vulnerabilities. This is like regularly changing the locks on your doors to keep intruders out.

Freeware options:

- Windows Update: Built-in tool for automatic updates on Windows systems.
- Software Update on Mac OS: Keeps Mac systems up-to-date with the latest security patches.

2. Continuous Monitoring: Implement continuous monitoring of your network to detect and respond to threats in real-time. Think of it as having a security guard who is always on duty.

Freeware options:

- Snort: An open-source network intrusion detection system.
- OSSEC: An open-source host-based intrusion detection system.

3. Multi-Factor Authentication (MFA): Use MFA to add an extra layer of security by requiring more than one form of verification to access accounts. It's like needing both a key and a fingerprint to unlock a door.

Freeware options:

- Google Authenticator: Free MFA tool for generating verification codes.
- Duo Mobile: Free app for two-factor authentication.

Investing in Ongoing Cybersecurity Education and Training

In order to keep cybersecurity procedures solid, ongoing education and training is essential. In order to keep your team current, follow these steps:

1. Regular Training Sessions: Conduct regular training sessions to educate employees about new threats and best practices. This helps them stay vigilant and informed.

Freeware options:

- Cybrary: Offers free cybersecurity training courses.
- Khan Academy: Provides various educational resources, including some on cybersecurity.

2. Phishing Simulations: Run phishing simulations to test and train employees on how to recognize and respond to phishing attempts. It's like running fire drills to prepare for an emergency.

Freeware options:

- PhishMe Free: Provides free phishing simulation and training tools.

3. Security Awareness Programs: Develop and implement ongoing security awareness programs that keep cybersecurity top-of-mind for employees. This is similar to having regular safety meetings in a workplace.

Freeware options:

- StaySafeOnline: Offers free resources and tips for cybersecurity awareness.

Partnering with Cybersecurity Experts

It may be particularly daunting for small firms to handle cybersecurity in-house at times. Collaborating with cybersecurity professionals can offer further assistance and knowledge:

1. Managed Security Service Providers (MSSPs): MSSPs offer comprehensive security services, including monitoring, threat detection, and incident response. They act like an outsourced security team, providing expertise and resources that might be lacking in-house.

Real-life example: A small legal firm partnered with an MSSP after experiencing multiple cyber-attacks. The MSSP provided 24/7 monitoring and response services, significantly improving the firm's security posture.

2. Cybersecurity Consultants: Consultants can assess your current security measures, provide recommendations, and help implement improvements. It's like having a security expert evaluate and enhance the safety of your home.

Real-life example: A small manufacturing company hired a cybersecurity consultant to audit their systems. The consultant identified critical vulnerabilities and helped the company implement stronger security controls.

3. Community Resources and Networks: Join local or industry-specific cybersecurity groups and forums to share knowledge and stay updated on the latest threats and solutions.

Freeware options:

- Reddit's r/cybersecurity: A community for discussing cybersecurity topics and sharing resources.
- LinkedIn Groups: Various cybersecurity-focused groups offer discussions, tips, and networking opportunities.

Your cybersecurity plan may be future-proofed by keeping up with new threats, being flexible, investing in your education, and teaming up with specialists when necessary. Maintaining the safety of your company in the face of ever-changing cyber dangers is possible with the help of these tactics.

It is critical for all businesses, no matter how big or little, to have a strong cybersecurity culture. It requires being proactive, learning new things all the time, and making good use of the resources you have. In order to protect your company from potential cyberattacks in the future, it is recommended that you implement the procedures described in this chapter.

These tactics are practical and inexpensive for small companies, and they are essential in today's digital age. To keep your business functioning efficiently and reduce the effect of cyber attacks, it is important to be proactive and prepared.

Chapter 10: A Step-by-Step Guide to Implementing a Strong Cybersecurity Policy

Because they usually have less robust security measures, fraudsters frequently target small firms. But to safeguard your company, you won't require complex or costly solutions. In this chapter, we will lay out the process for establishing a strong cybersecurity strategy, with an emphasis on employing freeware alternatives and practical measures. In this article, we will go over the most prevalent cyber risks to small businesses and provide you with easy measures to monitor for these attacks.

Step 1: Understand the Common Cyber Threats

Before implementing a cybersecurity policy, it's essential to understand the most common cyber threats that small businesses face:

1. Phishing: Fraudulent attempts to obtain sensitive information by disguising as a trustworthy entity in electronic communications.
2. Ransomware: Malware that encrypts data and demands a ransom for its release.

3. Malware: Software designed to disrupt, damage, or gain unauthorized access to a computer system.
4. Data Breaches: Incidents where sensitive, protected, or confidential data is accessed or disclosed in an unauthorized way.

Step 2: Develop a Cybersecurity Policy

A cybersecurity policy outlines the practices and procedures that must be followed to protect your business from cyber threats. Here's a simple framework to create one:

1. Define Objectives: Clearly state the purpose of the policy, such as protecting sensitive data, maintaining customer trust, and ensuring business continuity.
2. Assign Responsibilities: Identify who is responsible for implementing and maintaining the policy. This could be a specific employee or a small team.
3. Set Security Guidelines: Outline the specific security measures that employees must follow. This includes password policies, data encryption, and the use of antivirus software.
4. Create Incident Response Plans: Define the steps to take in the event of a cyber incident. This should include how to identify, report, and respond to threats.

5. Review and Update Regularly: Cyber threats evolve, so your policy should be reviewed and updated regularly to address new risks.

Step 3: Implement Basic Security Measures

Here are the minimum steps, processes, and software necessary to secure your computers, data, and network:

1. Use Strong Passwords: Ensure all employees use strong, unique passwords. Passwords should be at least 12 characters long and include a mix of letters, numbers, and special characters.
   Freeware Options:
   - Bitwarden: A free password manager that helps generate and store strong passwords.
   - LastPass Free: Another password manager that offers secure password storage and generation.
2. Enable Two-Factor Authentication (2FA): Add an extra layer of security by requiring a second form of verification to access accounts. Freeware Options:
   - Google Authenticator: A free app that generates verification codes for 2FA.
   - Duo Mobile: Another free 2FA app with additional features like multi-device support.

3. Keep Software Updated: Regularly update all software and operating systems to protect against vulnerabilities. Windows: Use Windows Update to automatically install updates. Mac OS: Use Software Update to keep your Mac up-to-date.

4. Install Antivirus and Anti-Malware Software: Protect your systems from viruses and malware.

   Freeware Options:
   - Windows Defender: Built-in antivirus and anti-malware software for Windows.
   - Malwarebytes Free: A free anti-malware tool that works on both Windows and Mac OS.

5. Use a Firewall: Firewalls help prevent unauthorized access to your network. Windows: Use the built-in Windows Firewall. Mac OS: Use the built-in macOS Firewall.

6. Encrypt Sensitive Data: Protect sensitive data by encrypting it, making it unreadable to unauthorized users.

   Freeware Options:
   - VeraCrypt: A free tool for encrypting files and drives, available for Windows and Mac OS.
   - BitLocker: Built-in encryption tool for Windows (Pro editions and higher).

- FileVault: Built-in encryption tool for Mac OS.

7. Regularly Back Up Data: Ensure that you have regular backups of all important data to recover quickly in case of a data breach or ransomware attack.
   Freeware Options:
   - Google Backup and Sync: Free tool for backing up files to Google Drive.
   - Time Machine: Built-in backup solution for Mac OS.

Step 4: Educate and Train Employees

Employees are often the weakest link in cybersecurity. Providing regular training can significantly reduce the risk of cyber incidents:

1. Conduct Regular Training Sessions: Educate employees on the latest threats and how to recognize and respond to them.
   Freeware Options:
   - Cybrary: Offers free cybersecurity training courses.
   - Khan Academy: Provides various educational resources, including some on cybersecurity.

2. Simulate Phishing Attacks: Test employees' ability to recognize phishing attempts by simulating attacks.
   Freeware Options:

     o   PhishMe Free: Provides free phishing simulation and training tools.
3. Create a Security Awareness Program: Develop an ongoing program to keep cybersecurity top-of-mind for employees. Freeware Options:
     o   StaySafeOnline: Offers free resources and tips for cybersecurity awareness.

Step 5: Monitor for Cyber Threats

Monitoring for cyber threats is crucial for early detection and response. Here's how to set up simple monitoring systems:

1. Use Intrusion Detection Systems (IDS): IDS helps detect suspicious activity on your network. Freeware Options:
     o   Snort: An open-source network intrusion detection system.
     o   OSSEC: An open-source host-based intrusion detection system.
2. Monitor Logs: Regularly review logs from your firewall, antivirus, and other security tools to identify potential threats. Freeware Options:
     o   Graylog: A free log management tool that helps analyze and monitor log data.
3. Set Up Alerts: Configure your security tools to send alerts for suspicious activities, such as

multiple failed login attempts or unusual data transfers.

Step 6: Respond to Cyber Incidents

Having a response plan in place ensures that you can quickly and effectively deal with cyber incidents:

1. Identify the Incident: Determine the nature and scope of the incident. This includes understanding which systems and data are affected.
2. Contain the Incident: Take immediate steps to contain the threat and prevent further damage. This might involve disconnecting affected systems from the network.
3. Eradicate the Threat: Remove the malicious software or block the attacker's access.
4. Recover: Restore affected systems and data from backups. Ensure that all vulnerabilities are addressed to prevent recurrence.
5. Review and Learn: Conduct a post-incident review to understand what went wrong and how to improve your security measures.

Step 7: Maintain and Update Your Cybersecurity Measures

Cybersecurity is an ongoing process. Regular maintenance and updates are essential to stay protected:

1. Regularly Update Your Cybersecurity Policy: Review and update your policy to address new threats and changes in your business environment.
2. Conduct Regular Security Audits: Perform periodic audits to assess the effectiveness of your security measures and identify areas for improvement.
3. Stay Informed: Keep up with the latest cybersecurity news and trends to stay ahead of potential threats.

Having a robust cybersecurity policy in place doesn't always need a lot of time or money. If you want to safeguard your small business against typical cyber dangers using realistic and affordable methods, this chapter is for you. The best way to keep your surroundings safe is to update your security measures, educate yourself often, and monitor your environment.

Integrating security into your business processes, providing continuing training and awareness, and successfully leveraging existing resources are all essential components of a sound cybersecurity culture. To protect your company from cyber attacks and keep it secure in the long run, it's best to be proactive and ready.

Conclusion

This book has covered a lot of ground when it comes to cybersecurity, from the significance of the topic to concrete ways that you can protect your small business.

Let's recap the key points we've covered:

1. Understanding Cybersecurity Basics:
   - Cybersecurity is essential for protecting your business from threats like phishing, ransomware, and data breaches.
   - Small businesses are often targeted due to weaker security measures.
2. Developing a Cybersecurity Policy:
   - A clear, comprehensive cybersecurity policy outlines the practices and procedures needed to protect your business.
   - Assigning responsibilities, setting security guidelines, and creating incident response plans are crucial components.
3. Implementing Security Measures:
   - Using strong passwords, enabling two-factor authentication, and keeping software updated are foundational security practices.

- Installing antivirus software, using firewalls, and encrypting sensitive data are additional essential steps.
4. Educating and Training Employees:
    - Regular training sessions and phishing simulations help employees recognize and respond to threats.
    - A security awareness program keeps cybersecurity top-of-mind for all staff.
5. Monitoring for Cyber Threats:
    - Continuous monitoring through intrusion detection systems and regular log reviews helps detect threats early.
    - Setting up alerts for suspicious activities ensures prompt responses to potential incidents.
6. Responding to Cyber Incidents:
    - Having a response plan in place allows for quick identification, containment, eradication, and recovery from cyber incidents.
    - Conducting post-incident reviews helps improve security measures and prevent future attacks.
7. Future-Proofing Your Cybersecurity Strategy:
    - Staying informed about emerging threats and technologies is vital.
    - Investing in ongoing education and partnering with cybersecurity experts can enhance your security posture.

As important as it is to maintain a robust and successful organization, cybersecurity is more than simply a technical point. Companies of all sizes confront the same challenges in today's global marketplace. You can safeguard your company without draining your money account if you know what you're doing and use the appropriate resources.

Think about a family-run internet store that was the target of several phishing attacks. They drastically decreased their vulnerability to these assaults by activating robust email filters, regularly educating employees, and utilizing two-factor authentication. By taking this preventative measure, they were able to enhance sales and expand their business while also protecting their customers' personal information.

Research shows that companies which invest in strong cybersecurity measures see a decrease in successful assaults and an improvement in recovery times. Case in point: data breaches are far less common at businesses that implement multi-factor authentication. Businesses that back up their data frequently can also recover from ransomware attacks with minimum inconvenience.

A nearby bakery has begun utilizing free security software such as VeraCrypt to encrypt sensitive client data and Google Authenticator to do two-factor authentication. Software update routines were also instituted, with the help of in-built utilities such as Windows Update and macOS Software Update. By taking these easy and inexpensive precautions, they greatly improved their security and could concentrate on expanding their business without being worried about cyber harm.

Establishing a solid culture of cybersecurity is crucial. Integrating security into your everyday operations, empowering and training your personnel, and regularly monitoring and upgrading your security processes are all part of it. This way, you can build a strong corporate culture where everyone knows their part to keep the assets safe.

After instituting a cybersecurity culture, a little marketing agency noticed a significant drop in security occurrences. Training sessions were frequently attended by employees, who took part in phishing simulations and adhered to best practices for data protection. Along with making them feel safer, this also encouraged them to work together as a team.

As a conclusion, cybersecurity is an essential factor in the success of small businesses. You can safeguard your company against cyber dangers, gain your customers' trust, and propel it to sustained success by following the advice in this book. Cybersecurity doesn't have to be hard or costly to be successful. Even small firms may attain a high degree of security and resilience in the face of emerging cyber threats with the correct mentality and tools.